LIVE ANCHORED

A BIBLE STUDY

Katie Robertson

"We have this hope [Jesus] as an anchor for the soul, firm and secure."

Hebrews 6:19

To order additional books, contact: katiejr@comcast.net

ISBN: 978-0-9979303-8-2

Inspira Literary Solutions, Gig Harbor, WA
Printed in the USA by IngramSpark, Nashville, TN

This book is dedicated to my daughter, Karina Jean — her life and faith are my inspiration to live anchored in Jesus and His truths every day.

TABLE OF CONTENTS

"In fierce storms," said an old seaman, "we must do one thing; there is only one way: we must put the ship in a certain position and keep her there." This, Christian, is what you must do.

Sometimes, like Paul, you can see neither sun nor stars, and no small tempest lies on you; and then you can do but one thing; there is only one way. Reason cannot help you; past experiences give you no light. Even prayer fetches no consolation. Only a single course is left. You must put your soul in one position and keep it there.

You must stay upon the Lord; and come what may—winds, waves, cross-seas, thunder, lightning, frowning rocks, roaring breakers—no matter what, you must lash yourself to the helm, and hold fast your confidence in God's faithfulness, His covenant engagement, His everlasting love in Christ Jesus."

Richard Fuller,
from *Streams in the Desert* by L.B. Cowan, April 1ˢᵗ reading

Preface

Several years ago I launched a women's group in Gig Harbor, Washington. We named it "The Anchor" and planned to meet monthly for worship and encouragement in our faith and friendship. I was planning the first talk and had been pondering how to explain to the women the anchoring points of my life and my faith.

One morning while running, head down in serious focus, I asked the Lord for some kind of confirmation of the anchor theme, an object lesson I could use. I wasn't thinking He'd give it to me right away; I was just thinking sometime. But when I looked up, right smack in front of me there was a sight so odd, yet amazing, it nearly took my breath away. It was a huge fir tree with a massive anchor chained to it! I have no idea how the anchor could have been placed there, given its size and weight. I had run this path countless times over fifteen years, so to only now notice what had surely been right in front of me all along was stunning. What a confirmation this was to me!

The shape of a strong anchor, with the image of a cross running through the middle, confirmed the five anchor truths that have guided my life:

1. **God loves you.**

   "For God so loved the world that he gave his one and only Son, that whoever believes in him shall not perish but have eternal life." (John 3:16)

2. **He hears you.**

   "Cast all your anxiety on him because he cares for you." (1 Peter 5:7)

3. **He never leaves you.**

   "And surely I am with you always, to the very end of the age." (Matthew 28:20)

4. **He never forgets you.**

   "Can a mother forget the baby at her breast and have no compassion on the child she has borne? Though she may forget, I will not forget you!" (Isaiah 49:15)

5. **He always holds you.**

   "So do not fear for I am with you; do not be dismayed, for I am your God. I will strengthen you and help you; I will uphold you with my righteous right hand." (Isaiah 41:10)

   These promises have held me secure throughout the various storms of my life. Many times, they were severely put to the test. I wanted to share these tried and true characteristics of God with the women at the Anchor because I want others to know He can be trusted, the way I've learned to trust Him. These truths are not just for me, but also for anyone who desires to anchor his or her life upon the solid rock of Christ. We can be confident in claiming these promises for ourselves, and teaching them to our children and grandchildren and anyone else God brings into our lives.

Coming upon this anchor on my run that morning, just as I was deep in prayer and seeking direction, was a significant "God moment" for me. I felt He was giving me that amazing visual experience as a way of showing me once again that He is real. He cares about what I have been through and was leading me into yet another opportunity where I could share His love and truth with others.

What are some of the storms you are facing now in your life? I hope you will find these truths to be as life-changing and confidence-building as I have.

Katie Robertson
Gig Harbor, Washington
July, 2017

"We have this hope (Jesus) as an anchor for the soul, firm and secure." Hebrews 6:19

"Oh, the joys of those who . . . delight in the law of the Lord, meditating on it day and night. They are like trees planted along the riverbank, bearing fruit each season. Their leaves never wither, and they prosper in all they do."
(Psalm 1:1-3, NLT, condensed)

"But blessed are those who trust in the Lord and have made the Lord their hope and confidence. They are like trees planted along a riverbank, with roots that reach deep into the water. Such trees are not bothered by the heat or worried by long months of drought. Their leaves stay green, and they never stop producing fruit."
(Jeremiah 17:7-8, NLT)

But the godly will flourish like palm trees and grow strong like the cedars of Lebanon. For they are transplanted to the Lord's own house. They flourish in the courts of our God. Even in old age they will still produce fruit; they will remain vital and green. They will declare, "The Lord is just! He is my rock! There is no evil in him!"
(Psalm 92:12-15, NLT)

Introduction

I often think about what it takes to get through the devastating losses of life. In our family's life, losing our 19-year old daughter, Karina Jean, to cancer in 2009 was the most devastating loss I'd ever experienced—and one I thought I could never bear. But with God's strength, we are standing strong, and God is more real to us all than ever before.

Through this difficult season, the metaphor of an anchor has become incredibly meaningful to me—and so very, very real. The scripture from Hebrews 6:19 that describes hope as being like an anchor for one's soul especially speaks to me. I know from owning a boat for many years how important the anchor is; it is not just a deck accessory. A boat's anchor, though small in size compared to that of the vessel, is heavy enough to hold firm in the midst of a strong squall, or storm. It is designed to grip into the bottom of the seabed so that even the strongest wind or current will not displace the boat or drive it onto the rocks. I find the comparison of hope to an anchor to be vivid and profound.

Life is full of stormy weather of varying degrees, from squalls to tsunamis. (I'm talking life circumstances, here—not meteorology.) As of this writing, I have walked with Jesus for more than 40 years. In those years,

I've experienced the exhilaration of clear skies and smooth sailing, and the anxiety and terror of high winds and stormy seas. Through it all, I've learned we need to have an anchor for our lives to keep us from being swept away, emotionally and/or spiritually, in any of the seasons of our lives. We have to set that anchor firmly in our hearts and begin to live and believe on the truths of God's Word.

Following are three things that are true of an anchor in the world of boating—and that are equally true in our everyday lives. Along with these truths, I've included some questions for you to reflect on as we get started in this study, and as you consider how to anchor your life to Jesus Christ . . .

1. **You *must* have an anchor.** It is required by law that every boat have one.

    Using boating as an analogy for life, what is your anchor? What do you tend to place your hope, confidence, and security on?

2. **The anchor must be properly set.** It is very important to think about where to set the anchor. Set the anchor of Jesus and His truths in your heart. The Bible tells us, "Above all else guard your heart for out of it is the wellspring of life" (Proverbs 4:23). The heart is where life starts so anchoring your life on God's truths will bring you life.

    Have you taken these truths from head knowledge to your heart? On a scale of 1 to 10, to what extent do you feel God's truths are set in your heart?

3. **Anchor in the calm before the storms hit.**

    Are you currently experiencing a time of calm right now, or a time of storm? In what ways are you experiencing this? (Note: It's best to anchor in the calm but never too late to anchor in the storm!)

It is when we are securely anchored that we can begin to live life to the full—REAL life. This is what Jesus promised when He said, "The thief comes only to steal and kill and destroy; I have come that they may have life, and have it to the full" (John 10:10). Living life on God's promises will keep us strong and keep us from drifting. We can stand firm and live life to the full now and for eternity!

> *"We have this HOPE [Jesus] as an ANCHOR for the soul,*
> *firm and secure."*
> Hebrews 6:19

Over the next five weeks, we're going to explore together what it means—and what it can look like—to live in an "anchored faith," one that is rooted and secured in the person of Jesus Christ, no matter what the conditions. Each week in your *Live Anchored* lesson, you'll have the opportunity to:

1. **Drop Anchor** – hear a story about how one of the five "anchor truths" became real to me, and what it can mean to you
2. **Check Your Bearings** – explore what God's Word, the Bible, says about that anchor truth and start to fill yourself up with truth
3. **Set the Anchor Truth in Your Heart** – apply the truths you are learning from God's Word to your own life so you can start to live in the abundant life Jesus promised us

When we are anchored to Jesus, we can endure, we can hold on to hope, and we can experience God's peace, no matter what the circumstances. I know. I have experienced it.

Losing our precious Karina at such a young age still does not make sense to us. Nor does it, on the surface, make God seem very good or loving. I get that. After all, I am human! Yet, despite the mental wrestling

I engage in at times with Him, in my core I know He is still those things. If I were He, I would have done things differently. Early on in Karina's illness, I thought it was a chance for Him to show His power so people could see and believe. But He did not choose to work that way.

Jesus said, "Unless a seed falls to the ground and dies it cannot bear fruit" (John 12:24). Yes, Karina did die, but it was only the shell housing her spirit that was freed in that instant to live on with Jesus. It is because of this truth that I want to tell the world about Jesus! He is the One who gave Karina and our family hope as she faced death. It was His peace and love that gave her the courage to live fully till the end, confident He would be there to meet her the moment she passed from this life to the next. She did not waiver in this belief, because over the course of her brief 19 years on earth a rock solid foundation of faith had been built, tried, and tested. Karina held to this tried and true fact: the God of the Bible is a God of hope and love despite what happens in life. Despite the pain, the hurt, and the agonizing separation of death, Jesus Christ is the real deal.

This is my truth as well, the anchor that holds me in the storm of that loss and any other trial that comes my way. Though ultimately He did not answer my prayers for Karina in the way I would have liked, He still showed His unfailing love to us over and over through many other answers and miracles, both large and small. He is still carrying us, and I trust in His ultimate plan.

I hope you will be encouraged as you work through this little study. My greatest desire is that you will catch a glimpse of Jesus Christ and His amazing love for you, and learn to trust Him as the anchor of your soul.

"And now, just as you accepted Christ Jesus as your Lord, you must continue to follow him. Let your roots grow down into him, and let your lives be built on him. Then your faith will grow strong in the truth you were taught, and you will overflow with thankfulness."
(Colossians 2:6-7, NLT)

WEEK ONE

God Loves You

For God so loved the world that he gave his one and only Son,
that whoever believes in him shall not perish but have eternal life.
John 3:16

Drop Anchor

Did you know that God is "dying" to LOVE on you? He literally sent His son Jesus Christ to die for you so your sin may be forgiven and you will have abundant life now and forever with Him!! He wants to be in a close loving relationship with each one of us, to guide and direct us in the best path specifically planned for each one of us.

I came to know Jesus when I was twelve years old, at a concert listening to Seattle pastor Wayne Taylor talk about God. Sitting in the front row apart from my identical twin, who was seated behind me for some reason, was a rare occurrence. We were usually inseparable. What she did, I did.

I usually followed her lead. But in this most sacred moment I was alone, just me, with my thoughts focused entirely on the speaker.

Pastor Wayne described how we can enter a personal relationship with Jesus Christ. He explained Him as "the way, the truth, and the life" (John 14:6). I had never thought about accepting Jesus Christ and having Him as my friend, and the prospect thrilled me. At that moment the voice said, "Katie, I love you, follow me." It was Him! The Lord Jesus was inviting me into a real and living relationship. Why hadn't someone told me this sooner?

I could hardly contain my excitement. In that moment, sitting by myself, not concerned about anyone or anything else, I stood up and chose to give my whole heart to follow Him for the rest of my days.

I realize this may sound fictional. The story of Christianity is fodder for skeptics and scoffers. But for those who have experienced His love, it is powerful and transforming. In that moment, I said yes to the voice and my "religion" was transformed into a relationship. That day marked the beginning of my friendship with Jesus. It is a friendship which has influenced every part of my life: my career choice, my marriage, my volunteer time, and my parenting. I have come to know God as a real person, someone who is interested in all that concerns me.

Check Your Bearings

I have never doubted God's love; He convinced me of it that first night. However, I have been plenty confused, at times, by why things happen the way they do. Many times things have not made sense, and Karina's death was one of them. But through the many difficult moments of my daughter's five-year cancer journey with leukemia, I saw God's love showered upon me and my family time and time again in special, significant ways. To this day, I continue to see His faithfulness, and His great love for us.

Read the following verses below in your own Bible. What do they tell you about God's amazing love?

John 15:9-17

_____

_____

_____

1 John 4:7-12

_____

_____

_____

Psalm 33:20-22

_____

_____

_____

Romans 8:37-39

_____

_____

_____

The reality is that nothing can ever separate us from God's amazing, unfailing love. No matter what you are facing in this life—or will face—God is going to show Himself to you in His special way! I like to say He knows your "love language" and will show His love to you in a very unique way (e.g., through special people, circumstances, etc.). His love is unfailing!

Set the Anchor Truth in Your Heart

The word "unfailing" means *never* ceasing, unending, and always dependable. I am constantly in awe of the way God's love is described in the Bible as "unfailing." Look at these verses below that speak about unfailing love. What do they say to you?

Psalm 13:5

_____

_____

_____

Psalm 51:1

_____

_____

_____

Isaiah 54:10

_____

_____

_____

Lamentations 3:32

_____

_____

_____

Psalm 33:22

_____

_____

_____

Think back on the past week or month . . . how can you see God showing His love for you? (e.g., a person He has brought in your life, help you've received, special circumstances, etc.)

_____

_____

_____

_____

_____

What do you sense Him telling you about Himself now, after reading these passages?

_____

_____

_____

_____

_____

ANCHORED

Week One Notes:

_____

_____

_____

_____

_____

_____

_____

_____

_____

_____

_____

_____

_____

_____

_____

_____

_____

_____

_____

_____

_____

_____

_____

_____

_____

_____

_____

He Hears You

Cast all your anxiety on Him because He cares for you.
1 Peter 5:7

Drop Anchor

I often share the story of the time I asked the Lord to help me find my daughter's little white headband that she tossed off her head when I was in Costco shopping one day. Karina was nine months at the time and I so enjoyed her darling look with a headband on. She was securely buckled in a backpack my husband carried and his last words before heading into Costco were, "She's going to lose that headband." I, of course, said she wouldn't! She just looked so cute and so we began our shopping.

Sure enough, at the checkout we noticed the headband was gone. We looked the store over—a daunting task considering Costco, of all places! After taking a look around the store once, I was determined a second time to find it. I knew it had to be there somewhere! So, I seriously asked the Lord to help me find it—I was confident that He is all knowing and could He just give me the eyes to find it?!

Soon after I had prayed those words I looked down and noticed what I thought was a white tissue or napkin wedged under some shelving . . . looking closer, I saw it was the headband! I really couldn't believe God cared for such a little detail of my life! I asked the Lord to help me find it and He led me right to it.

Check Your Bearings

He really does want us to "cast all our anxiety on Him," the big things AND the little things. He cares about them all.

What do the following verses say about how He hears you and cares for you?

John 1:12

_____

_____

_____

1 John 3:1

_____

_____

_____

Philippians 4:6-8

_____

_____

_____

Matthew 11:28

Proverbs 3:5-6

Set the Anchor Truth in Your Heart

When we come to faith in Jesus and receive and believe in Him, we become God's special children (John 1:12-13). He is our Father, and He loves each of us very much. He made you, specifically and purposefully. He has very special plans for you and cares about *all* the details of your life. You can come to Him with any concern, big or small.

The word "cast" in 1 Peter 5:7 means to "throw forcefully." You can throw all of your worries and anxieties on the Lord for He cares and loves you deeply! When you give your worries to the Lord, He will lighten your load and fill you with peace. You can come to Him with *anything* in prayer and then hold on to the truths and promises in His Word. It is not always easy, and it often comes down to a choice:

- Choosing not to allow fear and anxiety to control your life
- Choosing to guard your heart and live on the "anchor" truths
- Choosing to focus your mind on what is TRUTH in the midst of uncertain times

Let the words of Jesus in this verse sink deep into your heart: "Peace I leave with you; my peace I give you. I do not give to you as the world gives.

Do not let your hearts be troubled and do not be afraid" (John 14:27). Do you really believe these words? Ask the Lord to help these truths be set deep in your heart, and begin to live anchored no matter what you face in your life. **Remember: the Lord always hears you and cares for you.**

Can you think about a time when God answered your prayers? How did that grow your faith?

_____

_____

_____

_____

_____

What are some of the anxieties, fears, or concerns you are facing right now?

_____

_____

_____

_____

_____

What do the scriptures you read in this lesson lead you to do with those cares?

_____

_____

_____

_____

_____

I encourage you to take these scriptures and personalize them by putting your own circumstances in them talk to the Lord about them in prayer. Watch and believe, and wait in expectation as He answers you. Sometimes God doesn't answer the way we want. His plan for us isn't always what we think it should be—our Father knows best. His plan is way bigger and better than what we can imagine!

Devote yourselves to prayer, being watchful and thankful.
Colossians 4:2

ANCHORED

Week Two Notes:

He Never Leaves You

"And surely I am with you always, to the very end of the age."
Matthew 28:20

Drop Anchor

This became an anchor truth for me when I was a senior in high school and my first boyfriend broke my heart. I remember hearing the hurtful words he spoke as he broke up with me, but at the same time I heard a very gentle, soft voice in the back of my mind saying, "I will *never* leave you!" I knew it was the Lord reassuring me and bringing to mind the real truth of the matter and that was I was never going to be alone—no matter what—and that He would be with me. Many years later, this truth continues to bring me confidence, peace, and comfort every day.

Check Your Bearings

We live in a world with many "stormy" relationships. Family member betrays family member, spouses cheat on one another, friends argue— maybe you've experienced it, too, in one way or another.

It is encouraging to know that God never leaves or forsakes us. We sometimes forsake God but He never ever does us. Not only that, His love never fails and He never gives up on us! We do . . . He doesn't. The word "surely" that Jesus spoke in Matthew 28:20 means "for certain." You can rest assured!

What do the following verses say about the Lord never leaving you?

Joshua 1:9

_____

_____

_____

_____

Zephaniah 3:17

_____

_____

_____

_____

Deuteronomy 31:8

_____

_____

_____

_____

Psalm 23:4,6

_____

_____

_____

_____

Set the Anchor Truth in Your Heart

Can you think of a time you have felt very alone? Share about it and what brought you comfort.

_____

_____

_____

_____

_____

_____

_____

_____

_____

_____

Remember the Lord is ALWAYS with you and will never leave you. How does this anchor truth bring you comfort?

_____

_____

_____

_____

_____

Week Three Notes:

_____

_____

_____

_____

_____

_____

_____

_____

_____

_____

_____

_____

_____

_____

_____

_____

_____

_____

_____

_____

_____

_____

_____

_____

_____

_____

_____

_____

_____

_____

He Never Forgets You

"Can a mother forget the baby at her breast or the child she has borne?
Though she may forget, I will not forget you."
Isaiah 49:15

Drop Anchor

This became an anchor truth for me at a very difficult time in my life. Shortly after I had my third child, I fell into a time of postpartum anxiety/ depression. My life was out of control with a lot of changes—a move, my husband's job change, building a house, just to name a few. I didn't feel like myself and had lost the joy for life and wondered if I would ever feel normal again. I knew should be so happy with my two darling daughters and my brand new baby boy but I was overwhelmed! I really began to question my faith and wondered where God was—had He forgotten me?

Everything up to this point in my life had always been pretty smooth but now I was ready to be done with my faith. I continued to go to my Bible study even though at this point in my life I was just going through the motions. I am so thankful, though, that I kept with it, even at my lowest point. One morning, as the women in the study sat around me in a circle, I was holding my son to nurse him. We went around the circle reading a verse from our study, one by one. When it came to my turn, I could not believe the verse I was assigned to read. It was Isaiah 49:15—I had never read it before! The words spoke so clearly to me, "Can a mother forget the baby at her breast or the child she has borne? Though she may forget, I will *not forget* you!" Here I was, nursing my child. These words spoke truth to me, intimately and personally—a big anchoring moment in my faith.

Check Your Bearings

There are times in our lives that feel out of control and very stormy. We can feel alone and anxious, and wonder where God is. This truth is very important to live on: being confident that God is working in our lives and has amazing plans for us. We can hold onto to the truth that He will *never* forget us!

What do these verses below say about Him never forgetting us?

Jeremiah 29:11-13

Psalm 139:13-18

_____

_____

_____

_____

Isaiah 43:1

_____

_____

_____

_____

Ephesians 3:20-21

_____

_____

_____

_____

Set the Anchor Truth in Your Heart

Remember God's amazing love, care, and compassion for you. Lamentations 3:22-23 says, "Because of the Lord's great love we are not consumed, for His compassions _never_ fail. They are new every morning; great is your faithfulness."

Can you think of a time when you thought God has forgotten you?

_____

_____

_____

_____

_____

How did you feel?

_____

_____

_____

_____

_____

_____

And how do you feel now knowing that God doesn't forget you?

_____

_____

_____

_____

_____

_____

Week Four Notes:

_____

_____

_____

_____

_____

_____

_____

_____

_____

WEEK FIVE

He Always Holds You

"So do not fear, for I am with you; do not be dismayed for I am your God.
I will strengthen you and help you;
I will uphold you with my righteous right hand."
Isaiah 41:10

Drop Anchor

This anchor truth became tremendously real for me when Karina, at 19 years old, was diagnosed with leukemia for the third time. We were given the news late in the night at the hospital and I crawled into the bed with her. We snuggled up with each other for comfort .

As we lay there in the dark room pondering this horrible news, we both sensed a great feeling of calmness come over us. We felt as if we were being held in God's giant hand and felt a peace that surpasses all understanding. I remember saying, "Karina, there is nothing we can do; the

Lord has us in His hands and He will carry us where He wants us." It was a sense of complete surrender and trust that came with an incredible peace. We completely and literally put our lives in His hands.

There have been many, many times in my life I've wanted to panic: relationships gone awry. Financial crises. Important decisions to be made. Things that don't go the way I've planned. The list goes on. Just like there is not smooth sailing on the ocean indefinitely, neither is there ever smooth sailing in our lives indefinitely. Storms will come; count on it. But they don't need to drive fear into our hearts. We can be confident, anchored in the truths that hold us strong!

Check Your Bearings

God is always holding you. This truth is so great to set in our hearts. We can be confident that He is at work in our lives—holding us and carrying us where He wants us.

What do these verses say about God holding you?

Psalm 28:9

_____

_____

_____

Psalm 73:23-26

_____

_____

_____

Isaiah 49:16

_____

_____

_____

Psalm 63:8

_____

_____

_____

Set the Anchor Truth in Your Heart

Why should we fear when we are in God's hands, the creator of the universe? He will guide you through every tough situation and direct you on the right path. He wants our complete trust and dependence to be on Him.

I like to picture myself nestled in the giant palm of His hand, completely at rest and letting Him carry me where He wants me. He has proved Himself faithful over and over again.

Can you think of a time when the Lord has held you or carried you through difficult circumstances?

_____

_____

_____

_____

_____

_____

When you think of any "storms" you are currently experiencing, how can entrusting yourself to God's hands make a difference in the way you approach or experience them?

_____

_____

_____

_____

_____

_____

_____

Week Five Notes:

_____

_____

_____

_____

_____

_____

_____

_____

_____

_____

_____

_____

_____

End of Study Wrap-Up

For the four weeks prior to my daughter Karina's death, I spent my nights next to her bed in the hospital, sleeping on a little cot. We were like soldiers together in the trenches, fighting what was beginning to feel like a losing battle.

One night Karina awoke abruptly, waking me with urgency in her voice. "Mom", she said, "I see something. I think it's a metaphor."

Drowsy and skeptical, I replied, "Really? A metaphor? At two in the morning?" (My daughter didn't usually talk about metaphors so this really caught my attention.)

"Well, I see a tree," she explained, "It's standing tall and strong. All around it there's a storm and the other trees are whipping in the wind, but this one is standing strong."

As I listened intently, I envisioned a big fir tree standing tall amid a forest of other wispy trees blowing around and becoming uprooted. *There must be a meaning to this,* I thought. I had come to believe that God often gives dreams and visions to alert us as to what lies ahead. Given that Karina had been so sick yet seemed so coherent in retelling this vision, I wanted to take it seriously. I reasoned the tree that was standing firm must signify her in her fight against cancer. Surely she was going to come out of this storm standing strong. The winds of cancer would try to uproot her, but she would survive and not be felled, or so I thought.

Of course as the end drew closer and we finally lost her, I realized the metaphor was not about Karina living, but rather about staying anchored in faith amid the storms. The tree in her vision really stands for rooted faith. Cancer was her storm, but it did not uproot her faith. Instead, that faith carried her through the storm and into the arms of her Savior, Jesus.

My storm has been losing my beloved daughter. The storm of loss is like the strongest of winds. It can potentially devastate those who are left behind, but I too, am determined to stay anchored in the certainty of God's love and plan for me. When I run along my neighborhood route, I see a tree that stands out to me amid the 190 others. It is tall and strong and chained with an enormous anchor. It is fresh and free and always reminds me of Karina's words. Living anchored in Jesus, one will stand strong amid the storms.

It is only by standing firm on the hope of Christ that I can endure and press on. I felt she somehow knew this and was giving me encouragement for life even as she lay dying. Colossians 2:6 came to mind as I reflected on her vision: *"So then, just as you received Christ Jesus as Lord, continue to live in him, rooted and built up in him, strengthened in the faith... and overflowing with thankfulness."*

Staying on Course

As we finish this study I hope and pray you have been able to let some or all of these truths settle more deeply in your hearts. It is my prayer that you may experience the amazing joy and abundant life living anchored in Jesus and His love, truths, and promises.

Below are a few questions I encourage you take some time with after completing this study. Really press deep into your own heart—your emotions, your thoughts, your decision-making arena, your priorities and values—everything. Follow up with some others in your group. Share answers, and pray for one another as you each commit to living anchored in Jesus.

"And now, just as you accepted Christ Jesus as your Lord, you must continue to follow him. Let your roots grow down into him, and let your lives be built on him. Then your faith will grow strong in the truth you were taught, and you will overflow with thankfulness."
(Colossians 2:6-7, NLT)

What anchors you amidst the storms of life?

_____

_____

_____

_____

_____

Which Anchor Truth is easiest for you to set in your heart?

_____

_____

_____

_____

_____

Which Anchor Truth is the hardest for you to set in your heart?

_____

_____

_____

_____

_____

Is there a verse from this study that really speaks to you? Write it down here.

_____

_____

_____

_____

_____

_____

_____

_____

_____

_____

"I pray that from his glorious, unlimited resources he will empower you with inner strength through his Spirit. Then Christ will make his home in your hearts as you trust in him. Your roots will grow down into God's love and keep you strong. And may you have the power to understand, as all God's people should, how wide, how long, how high, and how deep his love is. May you experience the love of Christ, though it is too great to understand fully. Then you will be made complete with all the fullness of life and power that comes from God.
Now all glory to God, who is able, through his mighty power at work within us, to accomplish infinitely more than we might ask or think. Glory to him in the church and in Christ Jesus through all generations forever and ever! Amen."
(Ephesians 3:16-21)

ABOUT THE AUTHOR

Katie Robertson is a retired teacher who has devoted the current season of her life to speaking, mentoring, and serving in her community, bringing hope and inspiration for living a life anchored by faith in Jesus Christ. She founded and directs The Anchor, a growing intergenerational ministry to anchor women in faith and friendships, with locations in Gig Harbor, Snohomish, Bellevue, Kirkland, Edmonds, and Lakewood, Washington. A graduate of the University of Washington, Katie is also an artist, runner, and the mother of two grown children. Katie and her husband, Ron, live in Gig Harbor, Washington, where they continue to enjoy their seaside home and many adventures on their boat, the *Karina Jean.* They love to use their boat to serve; they are actively involved in leader care, hosting Malibu Couples Weekends, Young Life ministry, and benefits for a variety of local non-profits.

Also available:

Anchored
BY KATIE ROBERTSON

When diagnosed with cancer as a young teen, Karina Robertson was powerfully strengthened by her relationship with Jesus. Karina's story of unshakeable faith is told through memories, photographs, and the handwritten prayer journal entries of both mother and daughter. *Anchored* is a story for anyone seeking a renewal of faith, a model for anchoring a child in faith, or encouragement in their relationship with the Lord. It is a story about loving well, being loved, and trusting that—no matter what happens—we are in God's hands, anchored in God's unfailing love.

My Sister and Me
BY ANNIKA ROBERTSON

In this charmingly illustrated story, a little sister celebrates the fun of having a big sister. Real life little sister Annika Robertson wrote and illustrated this book at the age of 13 for her big sister, Karina, just after donating her stem cells, which were a perfect match for her sister's transplant to fight her cancer. A portion of the proceeds of this book goes to the Fred Hutchinson Cancer Research Center in Seattle, Washington.

Our Special Treasure
BY KATIE ROBERTSON

The story of a mother's and father's love for their "special treasure" introduces the young child to God's love and to His plan for each of us. Bright, cozy illustrations give a child's-eye view of what it means to be loved unconditionally, and each page of the story comes with a Bible verse. At the end of the book, young readers will enjoy meeting the real little girl who inspired the story, and parents will find tried-and-tested tips for anchoring a child in faith.

Available at Amazon.com

CPSIA information can be obtained
at www.ICGtesting.com
Printed in the USA
BVOW06s2156181017
497686BV00007B/9/P